Noah's Ark

and other Bible Stories

Retold by Vic Parker

Miles Kelly

First published in 2011 by Miles Kelly Publishing Ltd
Harding's Barn, Bardfield End Green, Thaxted, Essex, CM6 3PX, UK

2 4 6 8 10 9 7 5 3 1

EDITORIAL DIRECTOR *Belinda Gallagher*
ART DIRECTOR *Jo Cowan*
EDITOR *Carly Blake*
DESIGNERS *Michelle Cannatella, Joe Jones*
JUNIOR DESIGNER *Kayleigh Allen*
COVER DESIGNER *Joe Jones*
CONSULTANT *Janet Dyson*
PRODUCTION MANAGER *Elizabeth Collins*
REPROGRAPHICS *Stephan Davis, Ian Paulyn*

ISBN 978-1-84810-394-8

Printed in China

British Library Cataloguing-in-Publication Data
A catalogue record for this book is available from the British Library

ACKNOWLEDGEMENTS
The publishers would like to thank the following artists
who have contributed to this book:

The Bright Agency Katriona Chapman, Giuliano Ferri,
Mélanie Florian (inc. cover)

Advocate Art Andy Catling, Alida Massari

*The publishers would like to thank Robert Willoughby and
the London School of Theology for their help in compiling this book.*

Made with paper from a sustainable forest

www.mileskelly.net   info@mileskelly.net

www.factsforprojects.com

Self-publish your
children's book

buddingpress.co.uk

Contents

The Creation of the World

In the beginning, God lived in darkness. There was nothing else except for a vast ocean that rushed and raged over a mass of land that lay beneath. Then God had an idea. "Let there be light!" He said, and mysteriously there was. God liked the brightness. He enjoyed it for a while and then called the darkness back for another turn. That was the very first day and night.

When God lit up the second day He had another idea. "I want a roof to arch over everything, way up high!" He said, and all at once there was one. Then He parted the ocean, scooped up half of the water and poured it out onto the roof. The swirling patterns that formed above were beautiful. God gave the roof a special name – sky.

God looked down at the remaining water boiling and bubbling below. "Move aside so the land can show through!" He ordered, and it did. The land rose up and the water swirled around it. God was very pleased and decided to call them earth and sea. But He thought the land looked too bare. God imagined grass and flowers and bushes and trees. Before the third day ended, they were growing all over the earth.

On day number four, God decorated the sky. In it He hung a blazing, hot light called the sun, a pale, cold light called the moon and millions of twinkling stars. Then He set them all moving around each other in a way that would mark out the passing of the days, nights, seasons and years.

Next, God looked over His creation and decided that He wanted things to live in it. He spent the fifth day imagining all sorts of creatures that floated, swam and dived in the water, and that soared, hovered and buzzed in the air. Suddenly, the sea was filled with fish and sea creatures and the air was busy with birds and insects.

On the sixth day, God imagined creatures that galloped, hopped and

slithered. Creatures with fur, scales and shells, and with claws, hooves and horns. Creatures that barked, hissed, howled and grunted. All at once, the earth was alive with all kinds of animals.

Last of all, God took a handful of earth and modelled it into a figure that looked just like Him. He breathed into the figure's nostrils and it shivered, blinked and came alive. It was the first man, Adam.

God quickly realized that the man would be lonely all on his own, so He sent Adam into a deep sleep while He made him a companion. God gently took out one of the man's ribs. Then He shaped the rib into another, similar figure – the first woman, Eve. Finally, God brought Eve to life, then woke up Adam and introduced them to each other. God watched His two humans with delight. God was so thrilled with them that He put them in charge of all the other living things He had made. He even planted a beautiful garden especially for Adam and Eve to live in, in a place called Eden.

At last, God sat back and looked at the world He had created. He had used every colour, shape and texture, and every size, sound and scent that He could think of. God was very pleased and decided that He had done enough. He spent the seventh day relaxing after all His efforts. God ordered that from then on, every seventh day should be a special day of rest in memory of when He had completed His wonderful work.

And that is how the world was made.

Genesis chapters 1, 2

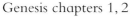

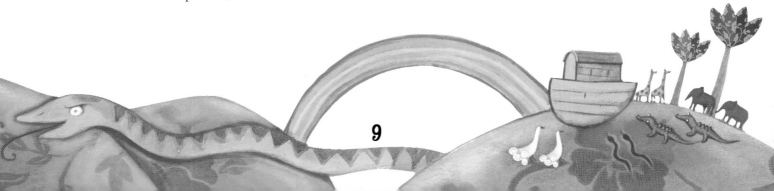

Adam and Eve in the Garden of Eden

God made sure that the Garden of Eden had everything that Adam and Eve needed to be happy. The sun kept them warm, so they didn't need clothes – they weren't embarrassed about being naked anyway. A gushing stream gave them water. All sorts of flowers, plants and trees grew there, fragrant and shady, and bearing tasty fruits, nuts and seeds. In the middle of the garden grew the two most beautiful trees of all – the Tree of Life and the Tree of Knowledge.

"Take care of my marvellous garden," God told Adam and Eve. "Enjoy eating anything you like, except for the fruits of the Tree of Knowledge. Please do not eat those. If you do, you will die."

Adam and Eve did as they were told and their life in the garden was wonderful, until one day Eve met a snake. The snake was by far the most cunning of all the creatures God had made. Very slyly, it asked Eve, "Did God really tell you not to eat from one of the trees?"

"Yes, that one," replied Eve, pointing to the Tree of Knowledge. "He said that if we do, we'll die. I don't think we're even allowed to touch it."

"Nonsense," hissed the snake. "You won't die! God doesn't want you to eat that fruit because if you do, you'll become like Him. You'll know the difference between good and bad, just as He does."

Eve gazed nervously at the Tree of Knowledge. How beautiful it was! Its leaves whispered mysteriously in the breeze and its branches stretched towards her. Its fruits hung down, ripe and ready to drop into her hand. "How wonderful it would be to become wise!" Eve murmured.

Overcome with longing, she reached out, picked the nearest fruit and took a big, juicy bite. It was so delicious! Surely something that tasted so good could not be wrong.

Eve hurried to share the fruit with Adam and he couldn't resist trying it either.

Suddenly, Adam and Eve realized that they did indeed know the difference between good and bad – and what they had done was very wrong. The couple felt dreadfully ashamed and were embarrassed about being naked too. They tried to sew leaves together to cover themselves. Then, in horror, they heard God coming. Quickly, they hid, but God knew.

"Adam," God called, "why are you and Eve hiding from me?"

The red-faced couple crept out, hanging their heads.

"We were frightened when we heard you, and also we weren't dressed," Adam mumbled.

"What has made you want clothes? And why are you afraid of me?" God demanded. "You haven't eaten the fruit I asked you not to eat, have you?"

Adam owned up, but he blamed it all on Eve, who in turn blamed the snake. God listened as they squirmed and squabbled. Then with huge disappointment He said, "I have no choice but to punish you all."

He sent the snake crawling away in the dust, the enemy of humans forever. After making animal-skin clothes for Adam and Eve, He turned them out of their beautiful garden home. "From now on, you will have to fend for yourselves and struggle to grow your own food," God told them. "And one day, you will go back to being the earth from which I made you – you will one day die." He set angels with fiery swords to guard the Tree of Life, so that Adam and Eve could not eat its fruit to save themselves from eventually dying. God watched in great sadness as the shamed couple walked out into the world.

Genesis chapters 2, 3

Noah's Ark

As the years went by, Adam and Eve had many great-grandchildren who had many great-great-grandchildren of their own. People spread all over the world. They quite forgot that they were part of one big family. They also forgot about God and began behaving badly in lots of ways.

God looked down from Heaven and

became more and more sad and angry. Eventually, people became so selfish and cruel that God was sorry He had ever created the human race. He decided the best thing was to remove everybody and start all over again.

Well, not quite everybody. There was just one person in the world who tried to live a good, honest, hard-working life – a farmer called Noah. God decided to save Noah, his wife and three sons, Shem, Ham and Japheth, and their wives.

God spoke to Noah and told him about His terrible decision. "Look around you, Noah. Everyone in the world is evil, and I have had enough. I am going to wash everybody off the face of the earth, but I promise, you and your family will be safe.

"Here's what you have to do. I want you to build a huge, covered boat – an ark. Use the best wood you can find and build it 133 metres long, 22 metres wide and 13 metres high, with a roof of reeds. Coat the whole thing with tar, inside and out, so that it is watertight. Give it a door and windows and build three decks divided into compartments. When I tell you, load up the ark with one pair of every living creature – a male and a female. Take seven pairs of animals you can eat because you'll need enough food to feed you all. I am going to send forty days and forty nights of rain to flood the whole world."

Noah told his family and they hurried to begin the enormous task. Their neighbours thought they were mad as they began building the huge ship. How people laughed! But Noah and his family trusted God and kept working, and after many months the ark was finished. The day came when God warned Noah to begin loading the animals into the ark and settling his family onboard. A week later, thunder clouds blackened the skies, blotting out the sun, and it began to rain.

Genesis chapters 6, 7

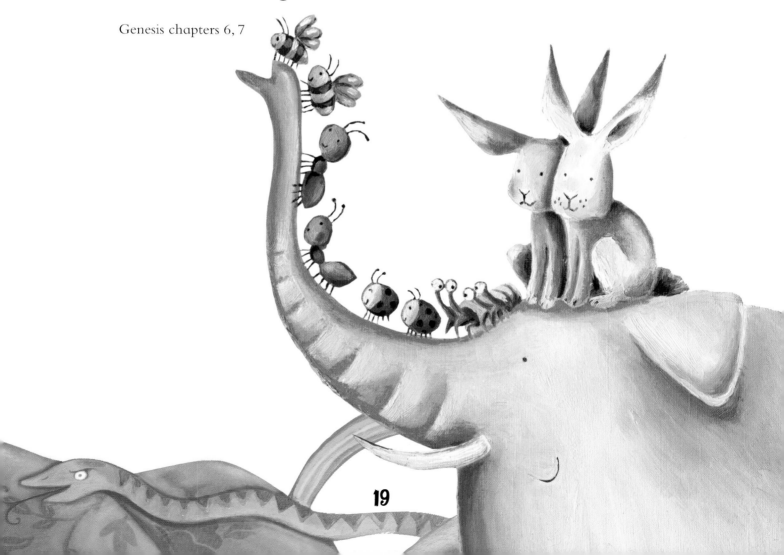

The Great Flood

The rain that God sent to flood the world was like nothing anyone had seen before or could have imagined. It was as if the sky had shattered and through the cracks plunged mighty waterfalls. As the rain poured down, rivers burst their banks, lakes flooded their valleys, oceans swelled and overflowed and the ark floated off on the rising waters. Towering tidal waves rushed over the land, drowning everything in their path, and still the rain continued. The ark was lashed and battered, and hurled this way and that by the currents.

The rain fell for forty days and nights just as God had said. Then as quickly as it had started, it stopped. When Noah dared to peep out, he could see nothing but water in all directions.

Over the quiet, empty days that followed, the sun began to dry up the water and the flood gradually started to sink. God sent a great wind to speed things along. Eventually, the ark groaned and shuddered as it scraped along the ground and came to a halt on top of Mount Ararat in Turkey.

Noah didn't dare leave the ark yet.

He waited a few days for the waters to sink further, then sent a raven into the sky. The raven soared back and forth and all it could see was water. Noah waited a week, then sent out a dove. It flew back the same day and Noah knew that there was not enough land showing yet. He waited another week, then sent the dove out again. That evening it returned, carrying an olive leaf. The waters were low enough to show land where trees grew! Noah waited one week more and again sent out the dove. This time it did not return. Nervously, Noah opened the door and the ark was surrounded by dry land!

Then God called, "Noah, it's time for you and your family to go out into the

world with the creatures and begin again."
And that's what they did. God was pleased
and blessed Noah and his family. He vowed
that He would never again send a flood to
destroy the living things He had created.
God set a rainbow in the sky as a sign to
always remind everyone of His promise.

Genesis chapters 7 to 9

The Tower of Babel

In the early days of the world people lived much longer than they do now. The Bible says that Noah was six hundred years old at the time of the flood and that he didn't die until he was nine hundred and fifty! Noah lived to see his sons and their wives have many children, grandchildren and generations of great-grandchildren.

The family grew so big that there were many thousands of people in the world again, just as God had wished.

Of course, people travelled to distant lands to find places to live. Many spent years wandering about, looking for good grazing land for their animals, living in tents that they moved from place to place. As time went on, people in different lands developed different tastes in clothing, cooking and customs, just like today. But one thing they all had in common was the same language.

When one particular group of wanderers arrived at the land of Shinar, which is now called Iraq, they decided to settle on a wide, flat plain. The countryside had everything the travellers could want, and they liked it

so much that they decided they would never move on again. The travellers thought hard and came up with a big, bold plan. Instead of living in tents, they would build a lasting home for themselves – a fixed settlement made out of bricks.

They worked out how to make bricks from mud, which they could bake hard and stick together with tar. But the people didn't want to build just a village or a town, they didn't even want to build a city. They wanted to build the grandest, most beautiful city with a tower for a showpiece. A tower so tall that its top would touch the clouds. The settlers wanted news of their magnificent tower and spectacular city to spread far and wide, so they would become known throughout the world. Dreaming of fame and fortune, they began to build.

With all the digging, moulding, baking, hammering and chiselling that was going on, it wasn't long before God noticed what the people of Shinar were doing. He looked down from Heaven and was amazed at the pleasing streets that were being laid out, the stylish houses that were taking shape and the stunning tower that was soaring upwards into the sky. "My goodness!" God said to Himself. "I can't believe what these people are achieving! They're doing a wonderful job."

But then a thought struck Him. "Hmmm… the only thing is, they're doing it because they want to be more important than everyone else. If I let them continue like this, they'll get quite carried away. Soon they'll want everything they have to be the biggest and best. I'd better put a stop to it before things get out of hand."

All at once, God gave the people different languages. Suddenly, they all found that they couldn't understand a word each other was saying. Without being able to communicate, their building plans ground to a halt. They couldn't work together to finish the city, which came to be known as Babel, or Babylon, because of the babble of voices inside it. Gradually everyone left Shinar in frustration and went their separate ways, seeking new homes.

From then on, as they settled in distant lands, people in different countries spoke different languages.

Genesis chapter 11

Abram's Journey

One of the descendants of Noah's son Shem was a man called Abram. He grew up in a city called Ur, near the Persian Gulf. After Abram married he took his wife, Sarai, his father, Terah, and his orphaned nephew, Lot (whom he had brought up as his own son) to live in a northern city called Haran. Both Ur and Haran were bustling

places full of wealthy people just like
Abram, who was a successful businessman.
But one day, out of the blue, Abram heard
God calling him.

"Abram, I want you to leave and go to
the country that I will show you. I am
going to make you the father of a great
race of people."

It must have taken a lot of faith to do as
God asked. Abram sold most of his
possessions, packed up the rest and set off
with his wife on a long journey without
really knowing where he was going. But
Abram did it without questioning and
talked Lot into coming too.

Abram bought flocks of sheep, goats and
cattle for himself and his nephew. He hired
shepherds too, and bought camels and

mules to carry tents, belongings, food and water. After weeks of preparation, Abram led his family and hired helpers away from everything they knew, moving in a huge train south.

God led Abram down into the land of Canaan, which is now Israel. When Abram reached a holy place called Shechem, he heard God's voice say,

"This is the country that I am going to give to your descendants." Descendants! He and his wife Sarai were well past middle-age and although they had always

longed for a family, they
had never been able
to have children.

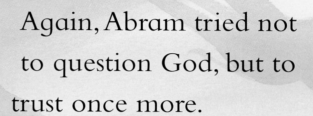

Again, Abram tried not
to question God, but to
trust once more.

They could not stay in Canaan as there
was a terrible famine, so God guided the
family through the desert to the lush land of
Egypt. Here, food and water were plentiful
but Abram found himself in quite another
kind of trouble. Pharaoh, the king of Egypt,
ordered that Sarai had to become one of his
wives. So God sent a terrible disease to
strike Pharaoh and his advisors until he
changed his mind, and he soon let Sarai go.

After that, Abram left Egypt behind and headed north into Canaan again, to a place called Bethel. There wasn't enough grassland for all the animals to graze on, and Abram's and Lot's shepherds began quarrelling and fighting over it. There was only one thing for it – the two men split up.

Lot went east into Jordan where he settled at a city called Sodom, while his uncle unpacked his tents and stayed in the countryside of Canaan. After Lot had left, God spoke to Abram again and repeated his vow. "Look around you," He said. "All this land as far as the eye can see will belong to you and your family forever."

And so Abram waited… Seasons came and went, but there was still no sign that he and Sarai would ever have children.

Over the years, God spoke to him several times, repeating his promise. It was always when Abram least expected it. One night, Abram was sitting outside his tent as usual when he heard God say, "Look up. You will have as many descendants as there are stars in the sky." Another time, after Abram had made an offering to God, he had a terrifyingly real dream. In it God walked right next to him, vowing again that he would have a vast, wealthy family and that all the land from the River Nile to the River Euphrates would be theirs.

As time went on, Sarai grew concerned that she would never be able to give Abram a child so she encouraged her eighty-six-year-old husband to have a baby with her maid Hagar, instead. Hagar and Abram had a son called Ishmael, but rather than cheering Sarai up, it plunged her into sadness.

Abram turned ninety-nine years old and Sarai reached ninety, and still they had no child of their own. However God insisted that His promise remained true. "I want you and your wife to change your names as a sign of my vow," He said. "From now on, you will not be Abram and Sarai, but Abraham and Sarah. Do what I say and trust me, and everything I have told you will come true. You and Sarah will have your own baby next year, you'll see. I want you to call him Isaac."

So Abraham and Sarah continued to wait.

Genesis chapters 11 to 13, 15 to 17

God's Promise Comes True

At long last, when Abraham was one hundred years old, Sarah had a baby boy whom they called Isaac. Everything had come to pass just as God had said.

The couple were so overjoyed that they thought nothing could spoil their happiness. But gradually, Sarah became eaten up with envy of Abraham's other son, Ishmael, whom he had with Sarah's maid, Hagar.

There had been trouble between the two women ever since Hagar had become pregnant. Because she was carrying Abraham's baby, Hagar had put on airs and graces and looked down on her mistress. Sarah had become so annoyed that she had treated Hagar badly. So badly that Hagar had eventually run away. An angel found Hagar weeping by a desert spring and comforted her, convincing her to return.

God reassured Sarah too. He said that He would make Abraham and Hagar's son,

Ishmael, the founder of a great race. But when Abraham and Sarah had a son, Isaac, it would be his descendants who would be God's own special people.

However when Isaac was born, the rivalry Sarah felt towards Hagar brewed again. Ishmael was about fourteen and he was fond of his little brother, but Sarah hated seeing them together. She couldn't stand to be reminded that because both boys had the same father, her maid's son was equally important.

"Get rid of them!" Sarah begged Abraham. "I don't want Ishmael around, taking what should rightfully be Isaac's."

Abraham was upset because he loved both his sons. He asked God what to do.

"Don't worry," God reassured him.

"Do as Sarah suggests. I'll look after Hagar and Ishmael. Trust me."

Next morning, Abraham told Hagar that she and Ishmael had to leave. With a heavy heart, he gave them food and a waterskin, and turned them out into the desert.

God kept His word and looked after Abraham's first son and his mother as they struggled to survive on their own. Once, when they were close to dying of thirst, God sent an angel to them with water. God stayed at Ishmael's side as he grew up, and he became strong and brave. Just as God had promised, He made Ishmael the founder of a great nation – the Arabs.

Genesis chapters 16, 17